THE **doors** UKULELE

Cover photo of The Doors in 1968 © Doors Property, LLC photographed by Paul Ferrara

ISBN 978-1-5400-9264-9

Visit Hal Leonard Online at
www.halleonard.com

Contact us:
Hal Leonard
7777 West Bluemound Road
Milwaukee, WI 53213
Email: info@halleonard.com

In Europe, contact:
Hal Leonard Europe Limited
42 Wigmore Street
Marylebone, London, W1U 2RN
Email: info@halleonardeurope.com

In Australia, contact:
Hal Leonard Australia Pty. Ltd.
4 Lentara Court
Cheltenham, Victoria, 3192 Australia
Email: info@halleonard.com.au

Alabama Song

Words by Bert Brecht
Music by Kurt Weill

why.   For   if   we   don't   find   the   next   { whis - ky
                                                          { lit - tle

bar, }   I   tell   you   we   must   die,   I   tell   you   we   must
girl, }

die.   I   tell   you,   I   tell   you,   I   tell   you   we   must

die.

Chorus

Oh,   moon _____ of   Al - a - bam -
(D.S.) *Instrumental*

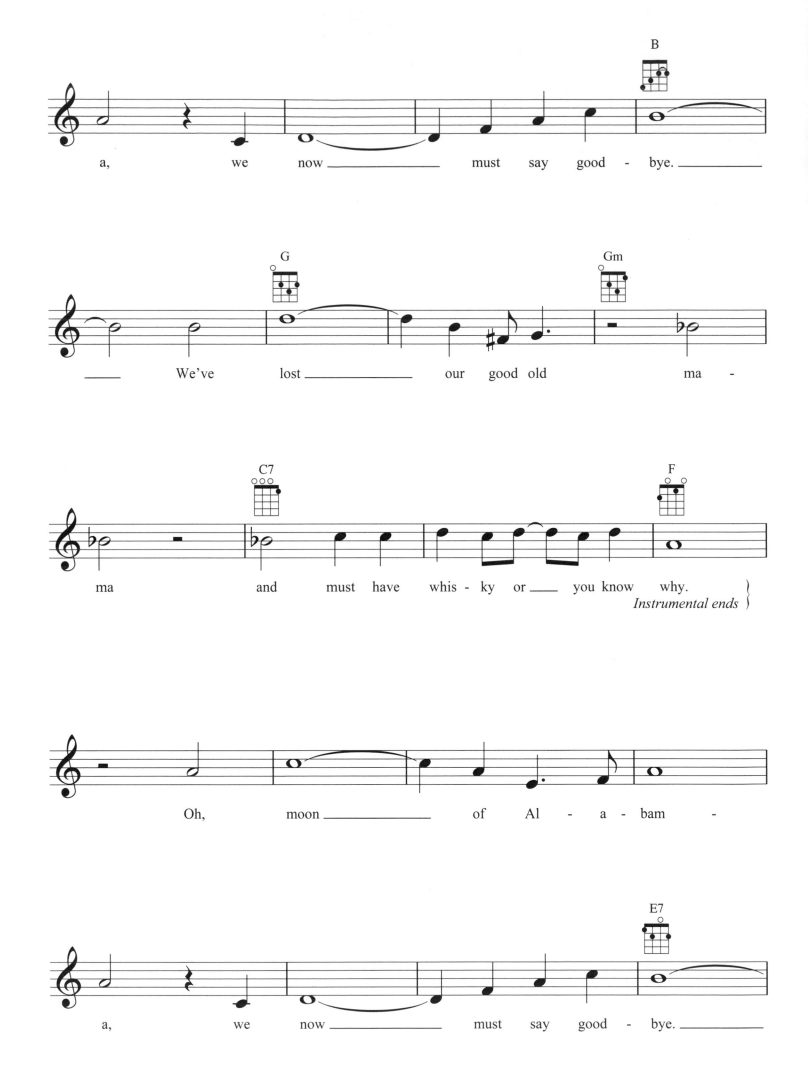

a,   we   now _____ must   say   good - bye. _____

_____ We've   lost _____ our   good old   ma -

ma   and   must   have   whis - ky or ____ you know   why.   *Instrumental ends*

Oh,   moon _____ of   Al - a - bam -

a,   we   now _____ must   say   good - bye. _____

We've lost _____ our good old ma -

ma, and must have whis - ky, oh, ____ you know

why, _____ yeah.

Verse

2. Oh, show me the way __ to the

D.S. al Coda

next _ lit - tle girl.

Coda

why.

Break On Through
(To the Other Side)

**Words and Music by John Densmore, Robby Krieger,
Ray Manzarek and Jim Morrison**

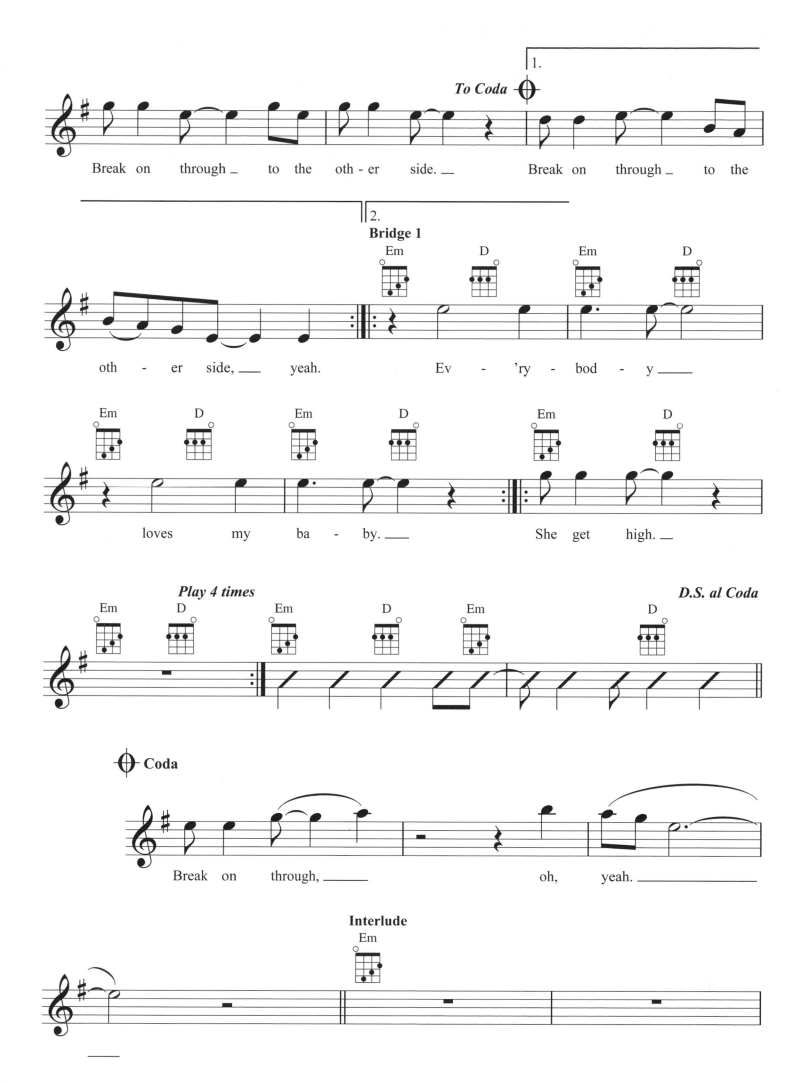

Bridge 2

Em

Made the scene __

week to week, __ day to day, __ hour to hour. __

D

Outro

Em

Gate is straight, __ deep and wide. __ Break on through __ to the

oth-er side. __ Break on through, __ break on through. __

Yeah, yeah, yeah, yeah. Yeah.

Hello, I Love You

Words and Music by John Densmore, Robby Krieger, Ray Manzarek and Jim Morrison

Chorus

Verse

The Crystal Ship

**Words and Music by John Densmore, Robby Krieger,
Ray Manzarek and Jim Morrison**

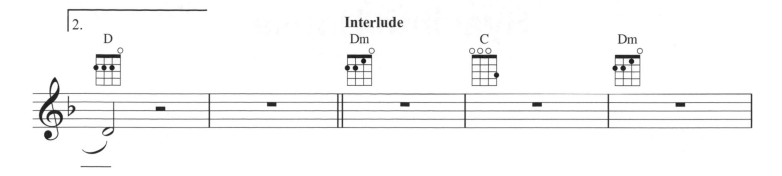

Interlude

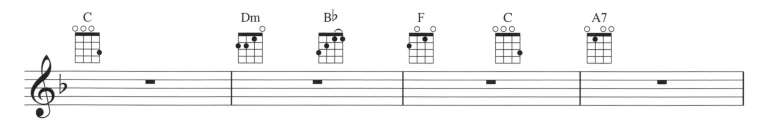

D.S. al Coda

3. Oh,

Coda

The

Outro

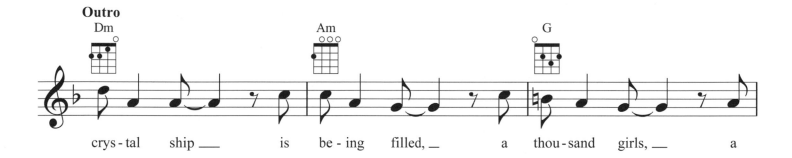

crys - tal ship ___ is be - ing filled, ___ a thou - sand girls, ___ a

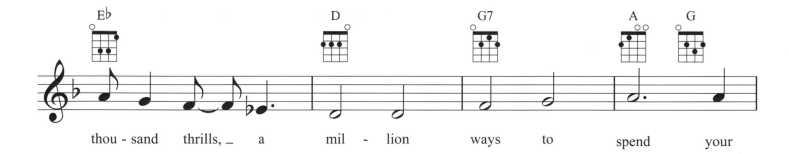

thou - sand thrills, ___ a mil - lion ways to spend your

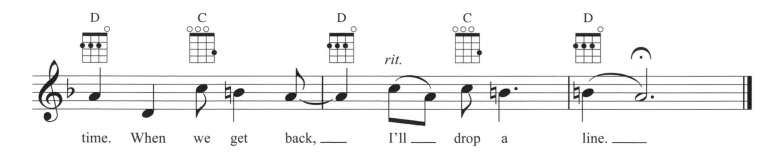

rit.

time. When we get back, ___ I'll ___ drop a line. ___

Hyacinth House

**Words and Music by John Densmore, Robby Krieger,
Ray Manzarek and Jim Morrison**

I need a brand-new __ friend __ who does-n't trou-ble me. __

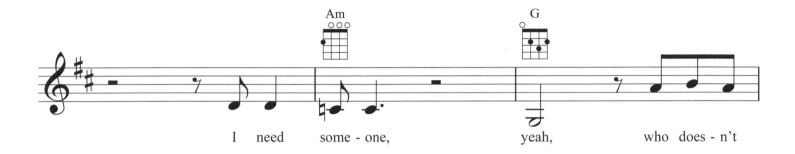

Am   G

I need some-one,   yeah,   who does-n't

D   **Chorus**
    Em

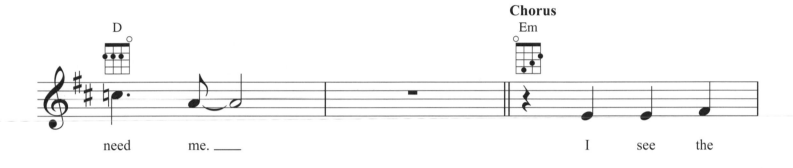

need me. __   I see the

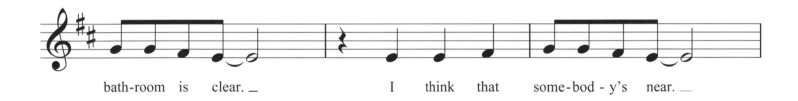

bath-room is clear. __   I think that some-bod-y's near. __

F#m

I'm sure that some-one is fol - low-ing me. _____

G   A7   N.C.

____   Oh,   yeah. __

Verse

D

3. Why did you throw the Jack of Hearts __ a - way? __

Why did you throw the Jack of Hearts __ a - way? __ It was the

Am   G   D

on - ly card __ in the deck that I ____ had left to play. __

And I'll

Outro

Am   G   1., 2. D

say it a - gain: __   I need a brand - new friend.

3.   D7   G   D

And I'll brand - new friend, __ the end. __

18

L.A. Woman

**Words and Music by John Densmore, Robby Krieger,
Ray Manzarek and Jim Morrison**

First note

Verse
Fast Rock

1. Well, I just got in-to town a-bout an hour a-go. __

Took a look a-round, see which __

__ way the wind __ blow.

Where's the lit-tle girl in the Hol-ly-wood bun-ga-low? __

Are you a luck-y lit-tle la-dy in the cit-y of light, ___

or just an-oth-er lost an-gel? ___

Pre-Chorus

___ Cit-y of night, ___   cit-y of night, ___

___   cit-y of night, ___

cit-y of night. ___   Whoa, come on!

Chorus

L. A. ___ wom-an,   L. A. ___ wom-an.

L. A. wom - an, Sun - day af - ter - noon. __

L. A. wom - an, Sun - day af - ter - noon. __

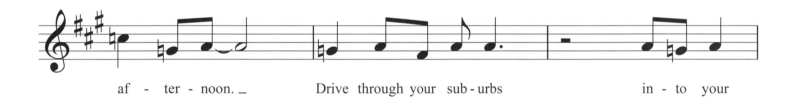

L. A. wom - an, Sun - day

af - ter - noon. __ Drive through your sub - urbs in - to your

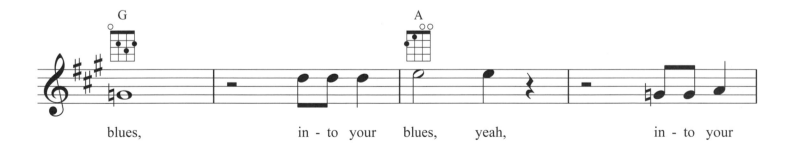

G   A

blues, in - to your blues, yeah, in - to your

G   A

blue, blue, __ blue, _____ in - to your blues. Oh, _____ yeah!

Interlude

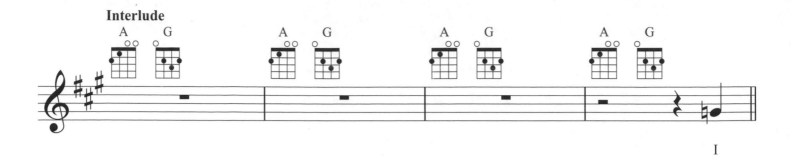

I

Bridge 1

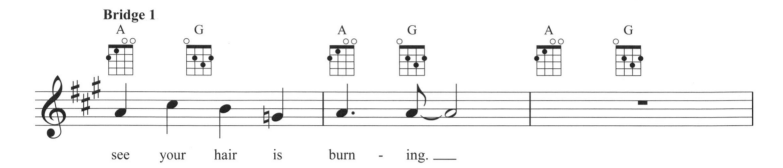

see your hair is burn - ing. ____

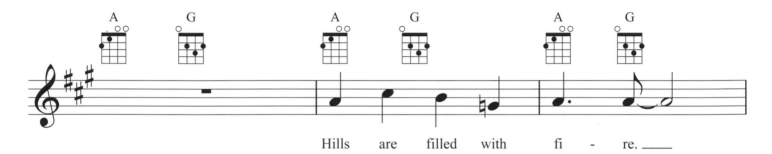

Hills are filled with fi - re. ____

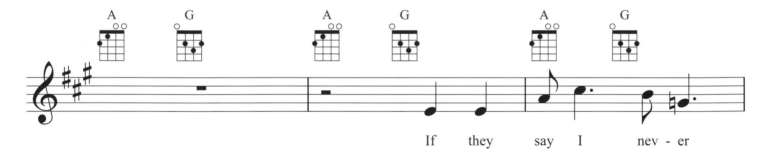

If they say I nev - er

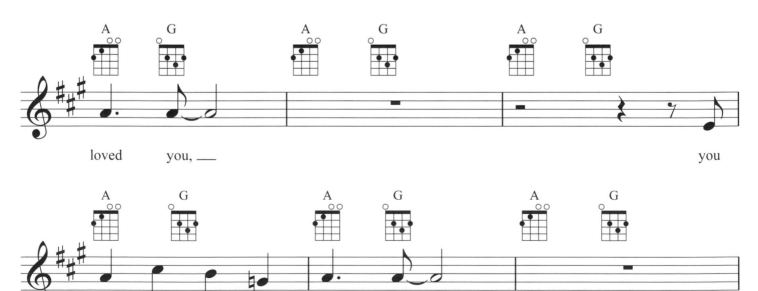

loved you, ____ you

know they are a li - ar. ____

22

Driv - in' down your free - way, ___

mid - night al - leys

roam.

Bridge 2

Cops in cars, the top - less bars, ___ nev - er saw a wom - an ___

___ so a - lone, ___ so a - lone, ___

___ yeah, so a - lone, so a - lone. ___

Mo - tel mon - ey,

mur - der mad - ness;

change the mood from glad ___ to sad - ness.

Interlude
Half-time

Bridge 3

Mis - ter Mo - jo ris - in', ___

___ Mis - ter Mo - jo ris - in', ___ Mis - ter Mo - jo ris - in', ___

_____ I got to rid - in', rid - in', _____ well,

Interlude
Tempo I (♫ = ♫)

A7

rid - in', rid - in'. _____ I got - ta, woo, yeah, rid - in'.

Verse

A

Oh, yeah! 2. Well, just got in - to town a - bout an

hour a - go. _____

Took a look a - round, see which __ way the wind __ blow.

Where's the lit - tle girl in the Hol - ly - wood bun - ga - low? _

Are you a luck-y lit-tle la-dy in the

cit-y of light, __ or just an-

Pre-Chorus
G

oth-er lost an-gel?_____ Cit-y of night, __

A

cit-y of night, __ cit-y of night, __

G A

_____ cit-y of night. __

Outro-Chorus
A

Repeat and fade

L. A. __ wom-an, _____ L. A. __ wom-an.
L. A. __ wom-an, _____ you're_ my __ wom-an.

Light My Fire

**Words and Music by John Densmore, Robby Krieger,
Ray Manzarek and Jim Morrison**

Love Her Madly

Words and Music by John Densmore, Robby Krieger,
Ray Manzarek and Jim Morrison

Don't you love her ___ face? ___ Don't you love her as ___ she's walk-ing out ___ the door ___ like she did ___ one thou-sand times be-fore? ___

Verse

___ 2. Don't you love her ways? ___ Tell me what you say. ___ Don't you love her as ___ she's walk-ing out ___ the door? ___

All your love, ___   all your love, ___

all your love, ___   all your love, all your

love is ___ gone, ___   so sing a lone - ly song ___

of a deep blue dream. ___   Sev - en hors - es seem ___

To Coda

to be on the mark.

Interlude

(Instrumental)

Verse

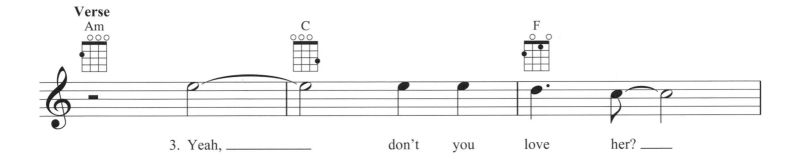

3. Yeah, _____ don't you love her? ____

Don't you love her as ____ she's walk-ing out ___ the door? __

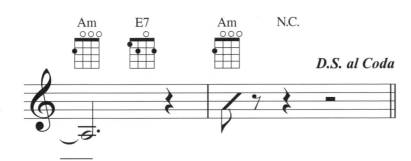

 Coda

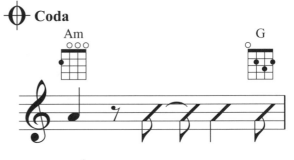

D.S. al Coda

mark.

Well, don't you

Outro

Repeat and fade

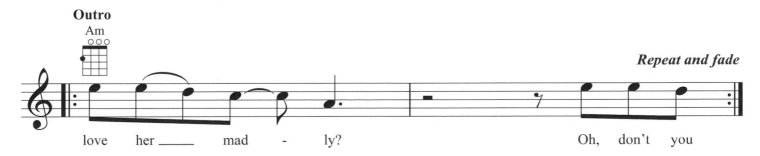

love her ____ mad - ly? Oh, don't you

Love Street

Words and Music by John Densmore, Robby Krieger, Ray Manzarek and Jim Morrison

1. She lives on Love Street, lin - gers long on Love Street. She has a house and gar - den. I would like to see what hap - pens. *(Instrumental)*

2. She has robes and she has mon - keys, la - zy dia - mond -

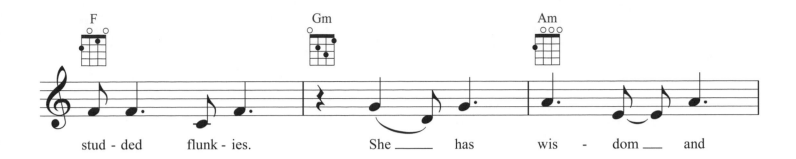

stud - ded   flunk - ies.   She ____ has   wis - dom ___ and

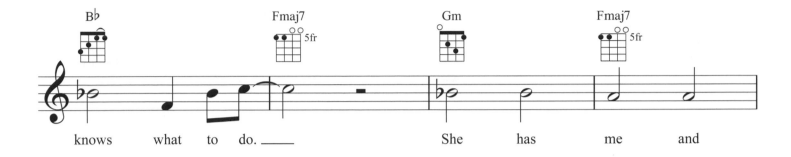

knows   what   to   do. ____   She   has   me   and

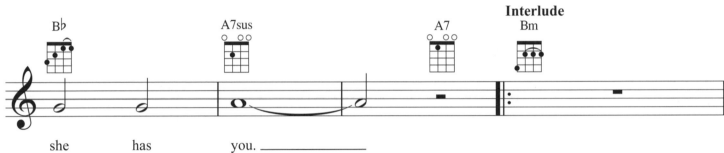

she   has   you. _____

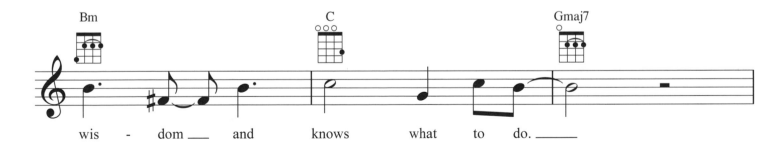

3. She _____ has

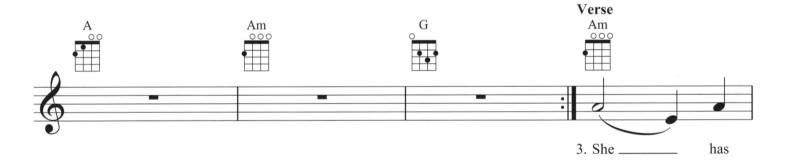

wis - dom ___ and   knows   what   to   do. ____

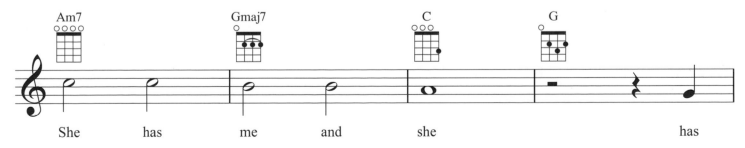

She   has   me   and   she   has

Interlude

you.

(Spoken:) I see you live on
I I wonder what they
I guess I like it

Play 3 times

Love Street; there's the store where the creatures meet.
do in there, Summer Sunday and a year.
fine so far.

Outro-Verse

She lives on Love Street, __
La la la la la __

lin - gers long __ on Love Street. __ She has __ a house __
la la la __ la la la. __ La la __ la la __

__ and gar - den. I would like to see what hap - pens.
__ la la la la la la la la la la la la.

Repeat and fade

Love Me Two Times

**Words and Music by John Densmore, Robby Krieger,
Ray Manzarek and Jim Morrison**

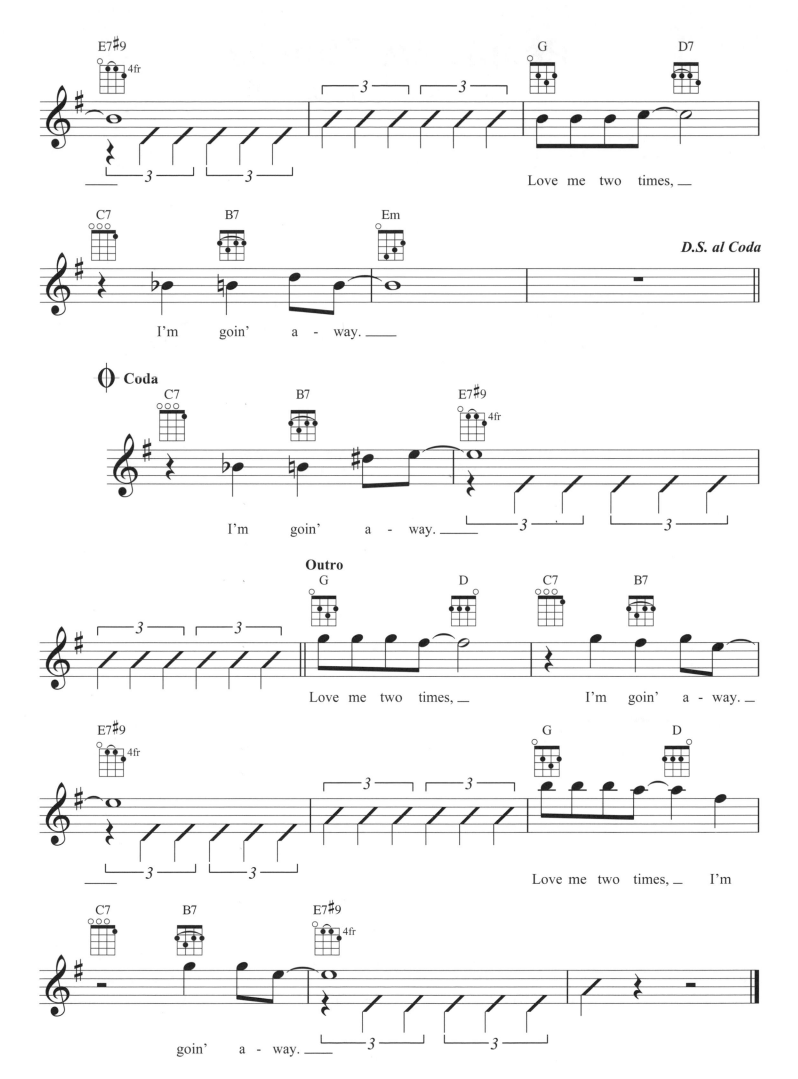

D.S. al Coda

Coda

Outro

Love me two times, __

I'm goin' a - way. ____

I'm goin' a - way. ____

Love me two times, __ I'm goin' a - way. __

Love me two times, __ I'm

goin' a - way. ____

People Are Strange

Words and Music by John Densmore, Robby Krieger,
Ray Manzarek and Jim Morrison

no one re-mem - bers your name. ___ When you're strange, ___

when you're strange, ___ when you're strange. _____

Verse

2. Peo - ple are strange ___ when you're a stran - ger,

fac - es look ug - ly when you're a - lone. ___ Wom-en seem wick - ed

when you're un - want - ed, streets are un - e - ven when you're down. ___

Interlude

When you're

⊕ **Coda**
Interlude

_Al - right, _ yeah._ _(Instrumental)_

When you're

Outro-Chorus

strange, fac - es come out _ of the rain. _ When you're strange, _

_ no one re-mem - bers your name. _ When you're strange, _

_ when you're strange, _ when you're strange. _

Riders on the Storm

Words and Music by John Densmore, Robby Krieger, Ray Manzarek and Jim Morrison

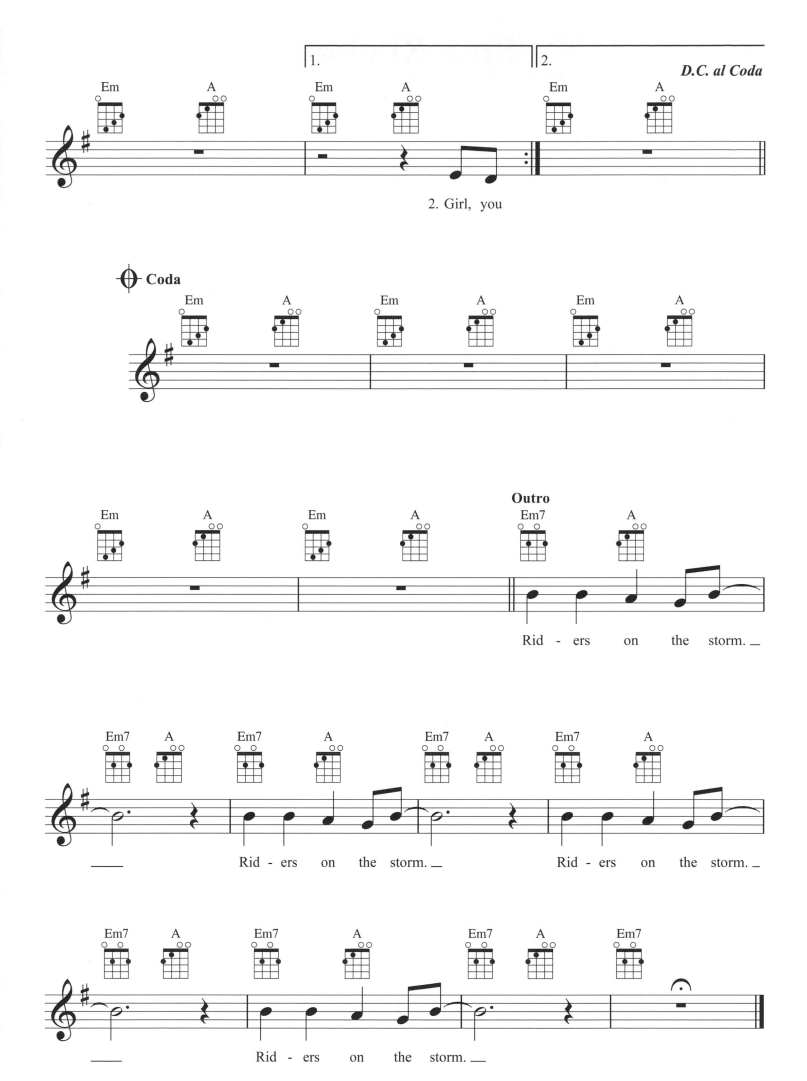

2. Girl, you

Rid - ers   on   the   storm. ___

___   Rid - ers   on   the   storm. ___   Rid - ers   on   the   storm. ___

___   Rid - ers   on   the   storm. ___

Soul Kitchen

**Words and Music by John Densmore, Robby Krieger,
Ray Manzarek and Jim Morrison**

First note

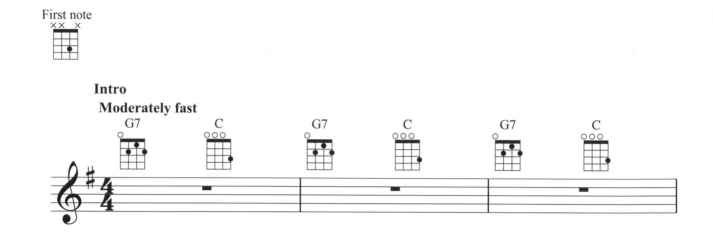

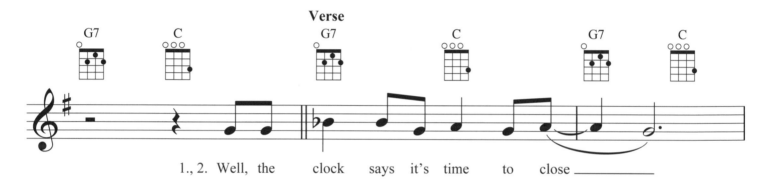

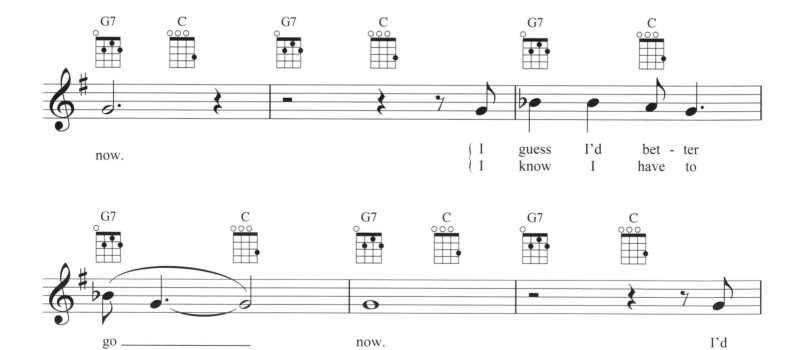

1., 2. Well, the clock says it's time to close _____
now.

I guess I'd bet - ter
I know I have to

go _____ now. I'd
go _____ now. I

Turn me out and I'll wan - der, ba - by, stum-bling in the ne - on

Bridge

groves. _____ Well, your fin - gers weave quick min - a - rets, ___

speak in se - cret al - pha - bets. ___ I light an - oth - er

cig - a - rette, ___ learn to for - get, _____

learn to for - get, _____ learn to for - get, _

_____ learn to for - get. _____ Let me

Waiting for the Sun

Words and Music by Jim Morrison

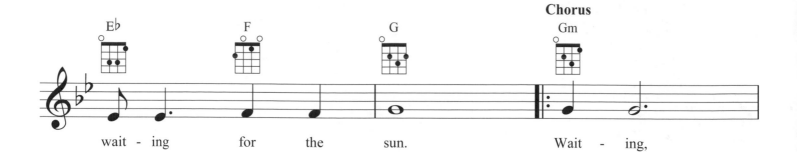

wait - ing   for   the   sun.   Wait - ing,

wait - ing,   wait - ing,   wait - ing.

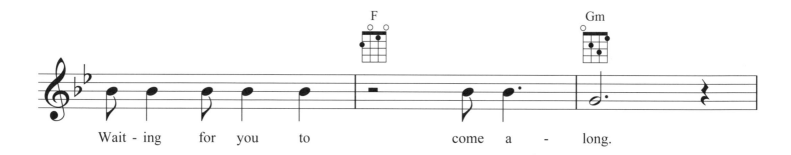

Wait - ing   for   you   to   come a - long.

Wait - ing   for   you   to ____   hear   my

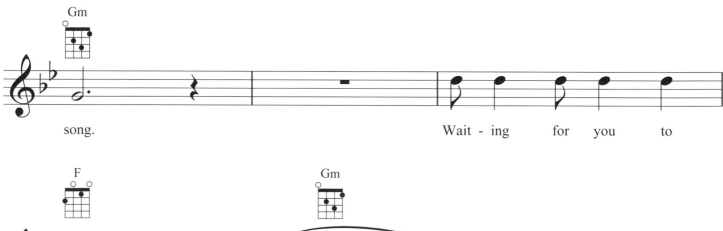

song.   Wait - ing   for   you   to

come a - long. _____

Wait - ing   for   you   to   tell   me   what   went   wrong. _____

Bridge

This   is   the   strang   -   est

life   I've _____   ev   -   er _____   known.

Interlude
N.C. (Dm)

Play 7 times   *D.S. al Coda*

(Instrumental)

Coda

wait   -   ing   for   the   sun. _____

Outro
N.C. (Dm)

(Instrumental)

Strange Days

Words and Music by John Densmore, Robby Krieger,
Ray Manzarek and Jim Morrison

we shall go on play - ing or find _____

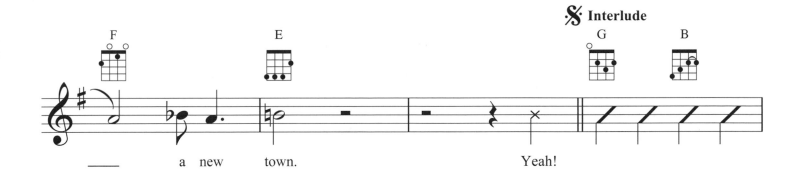

_____ a new town.   Yeah!

𝄋 Interlude

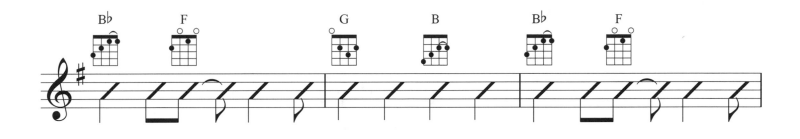

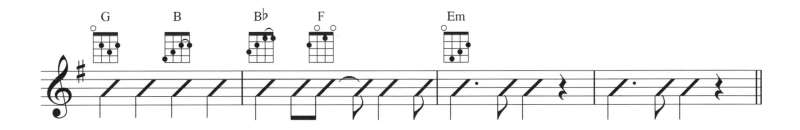

Verse

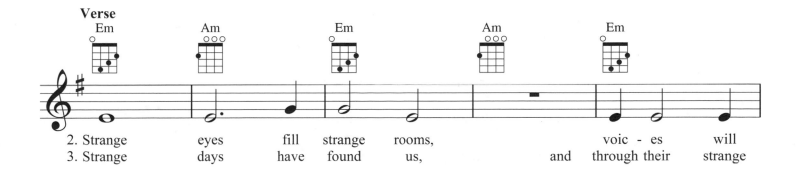

2. Strange   eyes   fill   strange   rooms,   voic - es   will
3. Strange   days   have   found   us,   and   through their   strange

sig - nal their ti - red end. The
ho - urs we lin - ger a - lone.

host - ess is grin - ning, _____ her
Bod - ies con - fused, _____

guests _____ sleep from sin - ning. _____ Hear
mem - o - ries mis - used _____ as we

me talk of sin and you know _____ this is
run from the day to a strange night _____ of

it. Yeah!

stone.

56